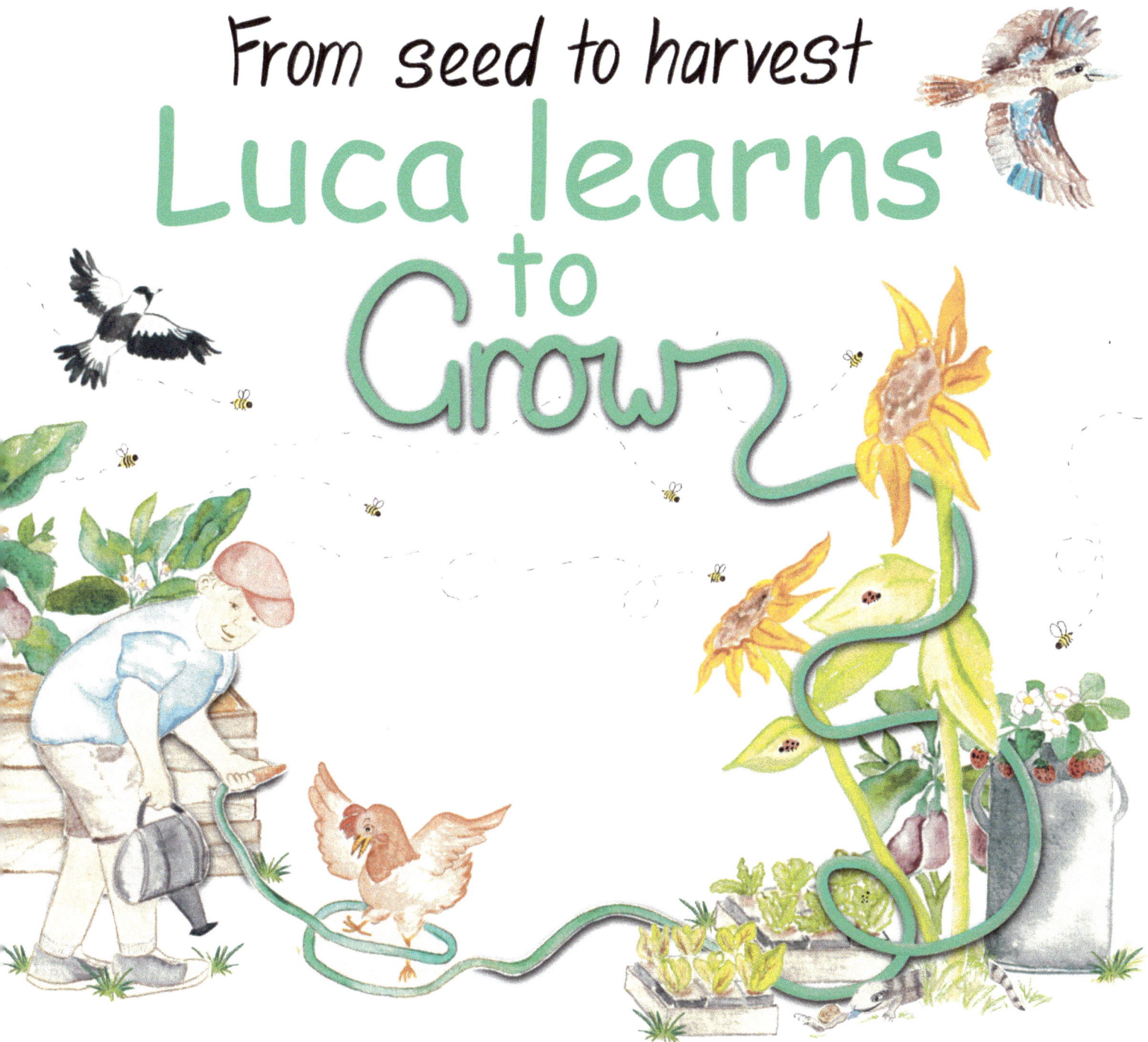

From seed to harvest

Luca learns to Grow

Leanne Murner

Illustrated by Natalie Herington

PLANETARY PRESS AND PUBLISHING
Fennell Bay, NSW, 2283 Australia

First published by Planetary Press and Publishing 2023
Copyright © Leanne Murner

Cover design and Illustrations© Natalie Herington 2023
Natalie Herington -Bird Valley Illustration & Design
Printed in Australia

ISBN 978-0-6456435-1-0

A catalogue record is available from the
National Library of Australia

www.planetarypp.com.au

Planetary
Press & Publishing

Dedication

I would like to dedicate this book to Nanny Cheryl for teaching and letting my kids explore and learn in your garden.

I would like to also thank my five boys Oliver, Luca, Franki, Loui and Leo.
Thank you all for being my inspiration and being on this journey with me.

Join Luca on a farm—tastic quest,
where veggies grow and critters nest.

Can you spot the fluttering birds,
crawling critters, and the sneaky blue
tongue hiding on each page?

Let the count and discovery begin!

HELP!

1

Today Luca is visiting Nanny on her farm.

Luca helps to gather all the seedlings from the green house, loads them onto the cart ready to plant them into the vegetable garden.

Dont eat me!

2

Luca has learned that all fresh fruit and vegetables in the grocery store have been grown on a farm like Nanny's.

In the orchard seasonal fruits grow on trees, like oranges, lemons, apples, pears, peaches, nectarines, bananas, avocados, and mangoes.

BUZZ BUZZ

3

I'm watching you!

4

In the vegetable garden carrots, potatoes and beetroots grow as roots under the soil.

Beans, cucumber, watermelon, pumpkin, and berries grow on vines.

Tomatoes, eggplant, zucchini, and capsicum grow on bushes.

Morning, friend!

Nice day, right?

6

Being a farmer is all about being sustainable in the garden. Some of the vegetable plants need to be left to go to flower. Bees and other insects will come and enjoy the pollen and nectar.

Once the flower is finished, the seeds will mature. This is a normal part of a plant's life cycle, producing seeds that will grow more plants next year.

8

Worms also help the vegetables grow. They travel through the dirt, making channels for air and water to flow through.

While they travel through the earth, they eat dead plants and leave poo behind. This nourishes the soil.

10

Worms can also live in a compost bin. Nanny puts her food scraps in here for the worms to eat.

The worms break down the scraps through their bodies leaving it in the soil.
This can then be returned to the earth as a organic fertiliser for the plants.

Yikes

11

Ahhh

12

What a
mess

13

Luca is digging little holes in the soil for the seedlings to be planted in.

He needs to make sure the holes are deep enough to cover all the roots of the seedlings, or they will dry out.

14

Our roof has solar panels, they supply power to pump the water.

Now the seedlings are in the ground they need a drink.

These are the water tanks that get filled from the rainwater that runs off the roof.

15

Luca should be watering the seedlings, not the chicken.

Not me!
The plants!

In the chicken coop, Nanny gathers up all the loose hay to put around the new seedlings. This will stop the ground from drying out.

Luca spots fresh eggs from the chickens, and they are still warm.

19

20

Luca finds a bee on a flower. Plants need bees to grow and produce food.

As bees stand on the flowers to drink their nectar, they get pollen on their legs. When they go to another flower, they transfer the pollen to that flower. This is called cross-pollination.

I wonder if that lizard is too big to eat?

21

In this bee hive the bee's go in the front and feed the babies with the nectar from the flowers.

All the excess nectar will be turned into honey.
We can then harvest it to eat.

Can you spot the Blue-tongue lizard?

23

Nice day for a
dirt bath!

Nanny doesn't use any nasty sprays or chemicals on the plants. She relies on the birds, bugs and reptiles to help keep the veggies safe.

This garden is its own little ecosystem. Everything works together to thrive.

I better hop out of here!

26

Luca puts all the seeds he gathered in a paper bag.

There is a whole collection of seeds here ready to be planted.

If you go to a Farmers market, you can meet the people that grow your food - and maybe even meet Nanny and Luca!

Hello!

Worm Wee $5

You are never too small to make a BIG Difference

Glossary

<u>Seedlings</u> - Vegetable seedlings are baby plants. They are planted in the soil, and with sunshine and water, they grow into the delicious vegetables we eat. So, when you see those little plants in the garden, remember, they're like the baby superheroes of our veggies, growing big and strong for us to eat.

<u>Green house</u> - Is made of clear walls and a roof that lets sunlight in, just like the windows in our home. Inside the greenhouse, it's warm and cozy, like a sunny day. Plants live in the greenhouse to stay safe and warm, especially during cold or rainy days. It's a magical place where plants can grow big and strong, no matter what the weather is like outside!

<u>Orchard</u> - An orchard is a special garden filled with trees that grow yummy fruits. It's a bit like a magical forest of fruit trees where you can go and pick delicious snacks right from the branches. So, when you visit an orchard, you're in for a tasty adventure.

<u>Seasonal</u> - Imagine fruits and vegetables having their own special time to grow and be the tastiest they can be. That's what we call 'seasonal.' When a fruit or vegetable is in season, it means it's the perfect time for it to grow and be picked because the weather and the sun are just right.

<u>Sustainable</u> - Sustainable means being a good friend to the Earth and taking care of our garden in a smart and kind way. In a sustainable vegetable garden, we make sure to use just the right amount of water, sunlight, and soil to help our plants grow strong and healthy. We don't waste things, and we recycle and reuse what we can. We also like to invite helpful insects and birds to our garden because they keep bad bugs away without using any chemicals. So, when we say our garden is sustainable, it means we're helping the planet and making sure we can keep growing yummy veggies for a long, long time.

<u>Crops</u> - Imagine rows of colorful vegetables and fruits like carrots, corn, strawberries, and more. These are our crops. We plant them, take care of them with sunshine and water, and watch them grow big and strong.

Channels - Channels are tiny tunnels that worms make in the soil. They wiggle and squirm through the soil, and as they move, they make these little paths or channels. These channels help air and water get deep into the ground, which is super important for the plants and trees to grow strong and healthy. So, think of worms as the garden's secret tunnel makers, helping the earth stay happy!

Compost - Compost is magic food for the soil in our garden. It's made from leftover fruits and vegetables, leaves, and even eggshells. We put them all together in a special pile, and over time, they turn into dark, crumbly, super-duper soil. This special soil is full of nutrients that help our plants grow big and strong. So, when we use compost in the garden, it's like giving our plants a yummy and healthy meal.

Water Tanks - A water tank is a giant, magical container that holds water for us to use. When it rains, the water goes into the tank and stays there until we need it. Then, when it's hot and we're thirsty, we can use the water from the tank to drink or water the plants in our garden.

Cross-pollination - Cross-pollination is a special way that flowers talk to each other in the garden. Pollen is like tiny, magical dust inside the flower. When the wind blows or bees and butterflies visit the flowers, they carry this pollen from one flower to another. They're helping the plants make new seeds so more plants can grow!

Harvest - Harvest is the day when we get to pick all the yummy vegetables we've been growing in our garden. It's like a treasure hunt, but instead of looking for gold, we're finding delicious carrots, juicy tomatoes, and crunchy cucumbers! When the vegetables are just right and ready to eat, we use our hands or tools to gently gather them from the plants.

www.ingramcontent.com/pod-product-compliance
Lightning Source LLC
Chambersburg PA
CBHW060753150426
42811CB00058B/1390

9 780645 643534